My Puppet Art Class

Nellie Shepherd

DK Publishing, Inc.

DK

LONDON, NEW YORK, MUNICH, MELBOURNE, AND DELHI

Editor Penny Smith
U.S. Editor Elizabeth Hester
Designer Wendy Bartlet
Managing Art Editor Diane Thistlethwaite
Production Rochelle Talary
Photography Stephen Hepworth

For Chris Harris (A Wonderful Person!)

ACKNOWLEDGMENTS
With thanks to: Jean Gollner, Anne Lumb, Wendy Morrison,
James Pendrich, Melena and Megan Smart (MMKS Logistics), Joan Fallows,
David Hansel (Memery Crystal), and the children from Cressbrook Mill,
Abbeydale School, and Broomhall Nursery School and Early Years Centre.
Special thanks to the artists: Peggy Atherton, Emma Hardy,
Donna Huddleston, Amy McSimpson, Lynne Moulding, and Emma Parsons.

First American Edition, 2003

Published in the United States by
DK Publishing, Inc.
375 Hudson Street
New York, New York 10014

03 04 05 06 07 08 10 9 8 7 6 5 4 3 2 1

Discover more at
www.dk.com

A catalog record for this book
is available from the Library of Congress.

ISBN: 0-7894-9855-3

Color reproduction by GRB Editrice, Italy
Printed and bound in Italy by L.E.G.O.

Where to find things

My Puppet Art Class

This book is all about making gorgeous puppets—and you can play with them, too!

The process of making and playing with puppets releases enormous amounts of imagination and creativity. It is a fantastic learning and developing experience! All the puppets have their own characters and personalities. My favorite pastime is 'swanning' around, so I love making Serena Swan best! Go for it!

Nellie Shepherd

Read Nellie's tips on page 46 and be inspired!

Basic Materials

As well as the equipment pictured with each project, you will need the following basic materials:

poster board	pots (for paint
construction paper	and glue)
paints	paintbrushes
felt–tip pens	rollers
pencils	tissue paper
glue	cotton balls
tape (masking	yarn
tape is best)	beads
scissors	
stapler	

Keep your art materials in a box so you can find them easily!

Helping hand

All the projects in this book are designed for young children to make, but they should only be attempted under adult supervision. Extra care should be taken when using sharp equipment, such as scissors, staplers, and pipe cleaners, and with small objects that may cause choking. Only use non–toxic, water–soluble glue.

Sidney Snake

stocking

button

My name is
Sss-Sidney.

felt

I'm a snake made from a stocking,
And I really love to charm.
I slither anywhere you want
When you wear me on your arm.

You can use...

glue

glitter

paint

shiny pieces

poster board

stocking or sock

buttons

felt

How to make it!

pull

Cut out a long strip of poster board slightly narrower than your sock. Pull your sock over the poster board. Now your sock won't stick together when you paint it.

paint

Mix paint with some glue. Paint zigzags, polka dots, stripes, or any other pattern on your sock to make your very own Sidney Snake. Glue on glitter and other shiny pieces.

glue

Glue on Sidney's red felt tongue and button eyes. Pull out the strip of poster board before your sock sticks to it.

play!

It's lots of fun playing with your Sidney Snake—and he keeps you warm, too!

8

Did you know? Snakes never stop growing. When their skin becomes too tight, they slide out of it. There is a new skin underneath!

Elsie the Elephant

paper plate

poster board

I'm Elsie
The Elephant,
And I love to play.
But that isn't very easy
When my ears
Get in the way!

You can use...

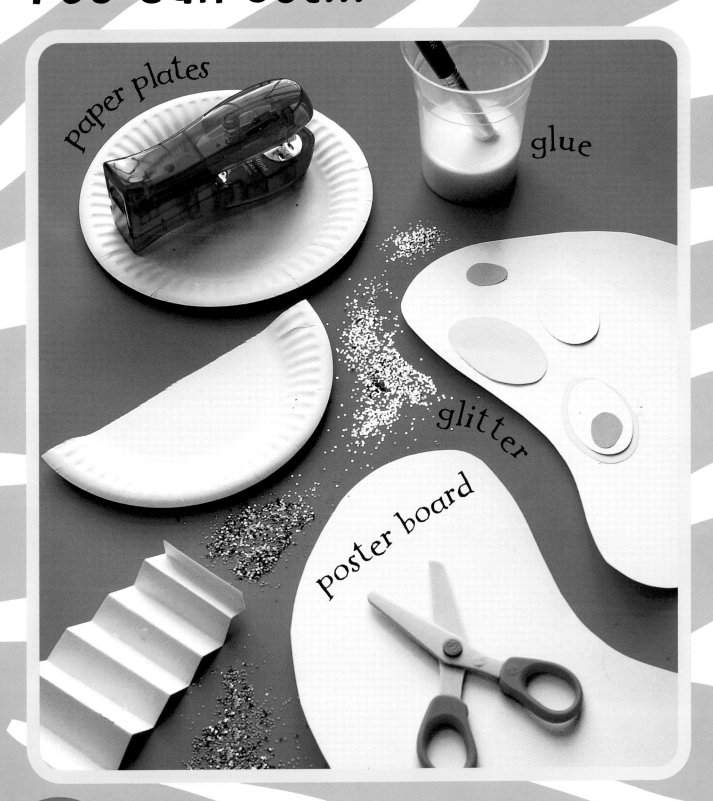

paper plates

glue

glitter

poster board

Tot Tip! Don't worry if you run out of paper plates. Just cut out a circle from poster board and use that instead.

Here We go!

cut out

Cut out two poster-board ear shapes like the one shown below. Staple them to a paper plate to make Elsie's head and her flappy ears. Staple half a plate to the back of Elsie's head, so it sticks out to make a handle.

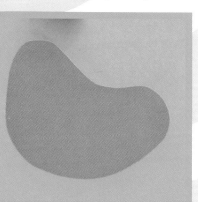

fold

Cut out a long trunk shape from poster board. Fold the poster board back and forth to make Elsie's accordian-like trunk.

glue

Glue or tape Elsie's trunk to her paper-plate head—her trunk bounces up and down! Glue on Elsie's poster-board face, and add glitter to make her sparkle.

Did you know? Real elephants like to flap their great big ears to help keep themselves cool!

Peter the Parrot

I'm a parrot called Peter,
With feathers very bright.
I'd love to be your friend.
Would that be all right?

paper fastener

I'm ready
to play
with you!

feathers

garden stake

You can use...

poster board

glue

tissue paper

coloured paper

glitter

paper fasteners

cork

wiggly eye

feathers

Tot Tip!

Use garden stakes to hold up your Peter Parrot. You can get them at a gardening store.

15

How to make it!

copy

Copy this picture of Peter onto poster board and cut it out. Cut out Peter's beak pieces and his wing separately.

Nice job!

stick

Brush glue over Peter's body and wing. Stick on multicolored paper shapes, feathers, and of course glitter! Make his eye from a cork and a wiggly eye. Decorate his beak, too!

attach

Attach Peter's beak and wing to his body using paper fasteners. Now these pieces can move up and down!

tape

Tape a garden stake along the back of Peter's body. Tape another stake along his wing and make him fly!

16

Kid's talk
"Parrots talk
a lot, just
like me."
Alex, age 3

You can use...

glue

rubber band

black fabric

yarn

poster board

pipe cleaners

shiny moon

garden stake

wiggly eyes

cotton ball

stars

Tot Tip!

For Mr. Sparks' body, you need to cut a cone from poster board and a robe from black fabric. Use the shapes below as a guide.

poster-board cone

fabric robe

You can do it!

glue

For Mr. Sparks' body, glue together your cone. Stick black fabric around the cone, leaving enough at the open end for his robe.

scrunch

Make Mr. Sparks' head by scrunching gluey tissue paper into a ball. Use more glue and tissue paper to stick the head onto a garden stake.

gather

Push the stake right through the cone. Gather the robe fabric under Mr. Sparks' head and secure it with a rubber band. Stick on his eyes, yarn hair, and cotton-ball beard.

wrap

For Mr. Sparks' arms, simply wrap a pipe cleaner around his body. To finish, glue on a moon and stars, a poster-board hat, and a little wand.

Kids' talk
"I pull the stick
and Mr. Sparks
goes away."
Sally, age 4

21

Kitty and Noodle

We're two little friends
Made from envelopes.
Our names
Are Kitty and Noodle.
Making us is lots of fun,
And when you're done,
You'll have a black cat
And a poodle!

straws

tissue paper

You can use...

glue

ribbon

glitter

envelopes

straws

wiggly eyes

tissue paper

poster board

Tot Tip!

You don't need new envelopes for Kitty and Noodle. Make them from old, used ones if you like—it's a great way to recycle!

Here We go!

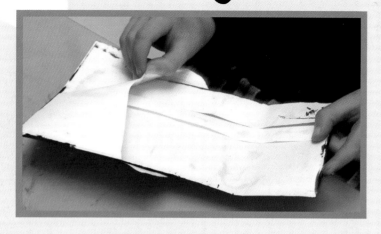

Kitty

For Kitty, slip one long envelope into a smaller one to make a 'T' shape. Secure it with tape. Then cut a strip off the bottom of the 'T' for your hand to go in.

stick

Stick on Kitty's poster-board ears, then paint her all over. Glue on eyes, a nose, and a mouth all made of poster board, and straw whiskers. We also gave our Kitty pink inner ears, a ribbon collar, and glitter!

Noodle

For Noodle, paint a long envelope in a lovely bright color. Cut a pointy chin shape at one end of the envelope.

cover

Stick on pieces of poster board for the top of Noodle's head and her ears. Cover them in tissue-paper balls. Stick on wiggly eyes, and use poster board for her eyebrows, nose, and mouth. Put glittery bows in her hair.

24

Serena Swan

I'm Serena Swan,
And I look very grand.
I swim around
So gracefully
When you wave
Your hand.

I like swanning around.

sock

feathers

paper plate

You can use...

glue

feathers

shiny shapes

pipe cleaner

wiggly eyes

felt-tipped pen

paper plates

sock

paint

flowers

tulle

Tot Tip!

For Serena's feathers you can cut a little bit off a cheap feather boa (no one will notice!) or use tissue paper instead.

How to make it!

tape

Put the sock on your hand and make Serena's beak by taping around your fingers. Use paint or felt-tipped pen to color her beak.

twist

For Serena's eyes, twist a pipe cleaner around her beak and stick a wiggly eye and shiny shape on each end.

staple

For her wings, fold four paper plates in half. Staple two of the plates together to make a bracelet that fits your arm. Staple the other two plates to the bracelet to look like wings.

play

Decorate Serena with feathers or tissue paper. We gave Serena a tulle headdress with little flowers. To play, pull on your Serena sock, slide the wing bracelet over the top, and have fun!

Kid's talk
"Swans are ducks
with long necks."
Clare, age 4

Bella the Butterfly

pipe cleaner

Kitchen brush

I'm Bella the Butterfly.
I flutter in the trees,
Then fly down to the flowers
To chatter with the bees!

paper plate

You can use...

glue

paper plates

pom-poms

glitter

paint

scissors

pipe cleaners

poster board

kitchen brush

tissue paper

sequins

Tot Tip! Instead of a kitchen brush, use a toothbrush to make a baby Bella the Butterfly. Cut out her mini-wings from poster board.

You can do it!

Fly high!

tape

To make Bella's wings, staple or tape together two paper plates. Then cut out two leaf shapes from poster board and tape one to each plate.

paint

Have fun decorating Bella's wings! Paint a pattern on one wing, then press the second wing onto the wet paint to make it match.

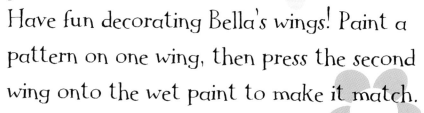

twist

Tape on a brush to make Bella's body. Twist on pipe-cleaner antennae and add a pom-pom eye on each.

stick

You can stick tissue paper to Bella's wings and add a tissue-paper fantasy tail. Glue on sequins and glitter to make her pretty. Then wave Bella up and down and watch her fly!

Kid's talk
"My butterfly flutters. It goes flut, flut, flut, when you shake it."
Helena, age 3½

Fingers and Thumbs

We're a group of puppet pals.
Come and check us out.
Put us on your fingers
And wiggle us about!

I'm a handy puppet.

fabric

Cheep!
I'm cheerful!

sequin

You can use...

glue

poster board

fabric

wiggly eyes

pipe cleaners

paper

pom-poms

shiny pieces

napkin

Boo!

Tot Tip! You can use all sorts of materials to make your puppets wacky and individual—yarn, paper, shiny beads and sequins, cotton balls, and lots more!

Here We go!

roll

Finger puppets are easy to make and so much fun to play with! To make a puppet's body, roll a rectangle of poster board into a tube that fits over your finger. Secure it with tape.

make a puppy...

There are so many ways to decorate your puppet's body—you can glue on cotton-ball fur, poster-board ears, and wiggly eyes to make a puppy.

I love that green hair!

...or a lady

Or try making a lovely lady by sticking on yarn hair, a bead mouth, and wiggly eyes. Add a fabric or napkin skirt held in place with pipe-cleaner arms.

make it up!

Here's a handful of puppets we've made. You can copy ours, or make up your own— and remember, anything goes!

Thumbs-up for me!

Kids' talk
"I've got friends
on my fingers."
Alex, age 3½

Bao Bao the Dragon

I'm lots of fun to make!

plastic fork

chopstick

paper plate

I'm Bao Bao the Dragon
And I come from China.
I dance up and down—
There's no dragon finer!

You can use...

glue

tinsel

glitter

paint

paper

paper
plates

chopsticks

plastic
fork

paper
fasteners

tissue paper

How to make it!

decorate

First, decorate five or more paper plates to make Bao Bao's head and body. Try using paint, glitter, or tissue paper.

Nice tinsel beard!

join

Join together your decorated plates using paper fasteners—attach the rim of one plate to near the middle of the next.

stick

Stick on Bao Bao's face—a tinsel beard and paper eyes, nose, and tongue work perfectly! Add horns and a tail cut from more painted plates.

tape

Tape on plastic forks to make Bao Bao's legs. Then make handles to hold by taping one chopstick to Bao Bao's head and another to her bottom.

Did you know?
In China, the dragon stands for long life and riches. People celebrate the Chinese New Year by performing with giant dragon puppets!

Show Time!

tissue paper

Squawk! Hi, I'm Peter!

cardboard box

Hello! I'm Serena Swan!

Now that you've
Got some puppets,
It's time
For you to know
How to make
A grand theater,
And put
On a show!

You can use...

glue

poster board

paint

tissue paper

string

clothespins

Tot Tip!

For this theater, you need two big boxes that are about the same size. If you don't have any, ask at your local supermarket.

You can do it!

cut

Your theater is made from two boxes stacked on top of each other. Cut the back and top off the lower box. Cut the front, back, and bottom off the upper box. Tape the boxes together.

cover

Cover your theater with tissue paper. Use a rag or roller to add lots of bright paint. Cut out a little peep hole in the lower box.

make curtains

To make curtains, run string across the front window of the theater and tape it in place. Fold tissue paper over the string and staple to hold. Slide the tissue-paper curtains along the string to open them.

finish

To finish, you can tape poster-board shapes to the top of your theater, stick on tissue-paper flowers, or clip on glittery clothespins. Then it's show time!

Kid's talk
"Don't sit on the boxes or you'll squash the play."
Max, age 3½

Nellie's Knowledge

I've been teaching my art class to children for over ten years. Along the way, I've discovered a few tips that make the classes lots of fun—and help bring out the creativity in all of us!

Organization
It's good to have all the things you need before you start. But if you don't have something, just improvise and use something else!

Make it last!
Use extra masking tape to give your puppets longer life. This tape is great—you can decorate on top of it!

Fun factor!
Think about inviting friends over to join in. Play music and have a story break. It makes such a difference.

Making mess
Art is a messy business! Just put down lots of newspaper, relax, and create. It's worth it!

Encouragement
Encouragement is great for building confidence and creativity: one hundred percent encouragement equals one hundred percent creativity!

Positive attitude
We're positive! In my art classes we never say we can't do something, because we simply can!

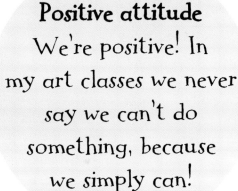

Making choices
Children's concentration is greatest when they choose the things they want to make. They make their own decisions from the start and they see them through.

Playtime!
Let children play with their art. It releases imagination and is the best fun ever!

47

We've had lots of fun. Curtain!